presented by:

# Crabtree Publishing Company
www.crabtreebooks.com

## To my own children, Celine and Nigel

**Coordinating editor:** Ellen Rodger

**Editors:** Carrie Gleason, Adrianna Morganelli, L. Michelle Nielsen

**Book design and production coordinator:** Rosie Gowsell

**Production assistant:** Samara Parent

**Scanning technician:** Arlene Arch-Wilson

**Art Director:** Rob MacGregor

**Photo research:** Allison Napier

**Prepress technician:** Nancy Johnson

**Photographs:** Leslie Garland Picture Library/Alamy: cover; Martin Harvey/Alamy: p. 23 (left); Roger Hutchings/Alamy: p. 15; qaphotos.com/Alamy: p. 26; AP photo/Keystone, Olivier Maire: p. 17 (top); AP Photo/Eric Miller: p. 27; AP/Photo/Jim Newman, University of Florida/IFAS: p. 17 (bottom); AP Photo/Michael Pobst: p. 19; AP Photo/NASA, National Snow and Ice Data Center, University of Colorado, Ted Scambos: p. 20 (top); LWA-Stephen Welstead/Corbis: p. 14; CP Images/AP Photo/Khalil Senosi: p. 25; Panos Pictures/Karen Robinson: p. 16; Philippe Bourseiller/Photo Researchers, Inc.: p. 20 (bottom); Chris Butler/Photo Researchers, Inc.: p. 18; Nigel J. Dennis/Photo Researchers, Inc.: p. 1; Gregory G. Dimijian, M.D/Photo Researchers, Inc.: p. 7 (both); Mark Garlick/Photo Researchers, Inc.: p. 21; Francois Gohier/Photo Researchers, Inc.: p. 22; Publiphoto/Photo Researchers, Inc.: p. 3, p. 13 (bottom); Carl Purcell/Photo Researchers, Inc.: p. 28; Peter Scoones/Photo Researchers, Inc.: p. 9 (top); Pasquale Sorrentino/Photo Researchers, Inc.: p. 8; Reuters/Greenpeace: p. 11; Reuters/Thomas Mukoya: p. 24; Reuters/Christinne Muschi: p. 29 (right); Copyright SEPM. Image courtesy – Society of Sedimentary Geology: p. 23 (right). Other images from stock photo CD.

**Illustrations:** Dan Pressman: p. 6, p.10; Chrissie Wysotski, Allure Illustrations: pp. 30-31

**Cover:** The cooling towers of a coal-fired power plant spew pollution that contributes to global warming.

**Title page:** A water reservoir is dried out after a prolonged drought.

**Contents:** Industrial smokestacks contribute to pollution and global warming.

**Library and Archives Canada Cataloguing in Publication**

Cheel, Richard James
   Global warming alert! / Richard Cheel.

(Disaster alert!)
Includes index.
ISBN 978-0-7787-1587-0 (bound)
ISBN 978-0-7787-1619-8 (pbk.)

   1. Global warming--Juvenile literature. I. Title. II. Series.

QC981.8.G56C44 2007    j363.738'74    C2007-900666-3

**Library of Congress Cataloging-in-Publication Data**

Cheel, Richard (Richard James), 1953-
   Global warming alert! / written by Dr. Richard Cheel.
     p. cm. -- (Disaster alert!)
   Includes index.
   ISBN-13: 978-0-7787-1587-0 (rlb)
   ISBN-13: 978-0-7787-1619-8 (pbk.)
   ISBN-10: 0-7787-1587-6 (rlb)
   ISBN-10: 0-7787-1619-8 (pbk.)
   1. Global warming--Juvenile literature. I. Title. II. Series.

   QC981.8.G56C423 2007
   363.738'74--dc22

   2007003403

## Crabtree Publishing Company
www.crabtreebooks.com    1-800-387-7650

**Published in Canada**
Crabtree Publishing
616 Welland Ave.
St. Catharines, ON
L2M 5V6

**Published in the United States**
Crabtree Publishing
PMB16A
350 Fifth Ave., Suite 3308
New York, NY 10118

**Published in the United Kingdom**
Crabtree Publishing
White Cross Mills
High Town, Lancaster
LA1 4XS

**Published in Australia**
Crabtree Publishing
386 Mt. Alexander Rd.
Ascot Vale (Melbourne)
VIC 3032

# Table of Contents

# Warmer and Warmer

Global warming is the gradual rise of the Earth's temperature. In some areas, the temperature has gone up by as much as 7 degrees Fahrenheit (or 3.8 degrees Celsius) over the past 50 years. This rapid rise has been linked to the way humans live today. Many scientists believe that Earth will continue to become warmer and endanger lives by changing environments and animal habitats.

## Climate change

Climate change refers to changes in long-term weather patterns throughout the Earth. Scientists are constantly studying climate change. There is much that they still do not know. What they do know is that the **glaciers** of ice that now cover much of the north and south poles, extended over much more of land and ocean surfaces 18,000 years ago. All that remains today are the **polar ice caps** and smaller glaciers in mountainous regions. With global warming will come the melting of the glaciers, and changes to the landscapes that are home to every living thing on Earth.

*What is a disaster?*
*A disaster is a destructive event that affects the natural world and human communities. Some disasters are predictable and others occur without warning. Coping successfully with a disaster often depends on a community's preparation.*

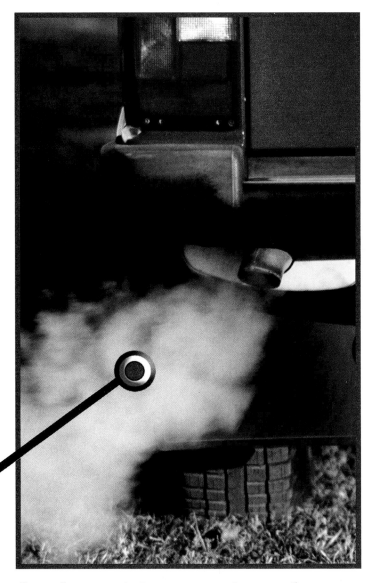

Car exhaust emissions are a major contributor to greenhouse gases, *which trap the Sun's heat in the atmosphere and contribute to global warming.*

## Fossil fuel pollution

Many scientists believe that humans have been at least partly responsible for the rising temperatures over the past couple of hundred years. Humans burn **fossils fuels** to power automobiles, heat homes, and produce electricity. Burning fossil fuels releases pollution in the form of gases that become part of the Earth's **atmosphere**. Scientists believe some of these gases cause global warming. Many countries are now working to find ways to stop global warming by reducing pollution in the Earth's atmosphere.

# Arctic emergency

The Inuit people of Greenland and northern Canada have lived in the Arctic for thousands of years. Traditionally, they survived with the help of their vast knowledge of weather and climate. Inuit elders, the people who pass on the stories of living on the land, have been frightened by recent changes in Arctic weather. The elders say it takes longer for the fall freeze to come and the winters are not as cold. Inuit traditionally used the stars, clouds, wind, water, and the way animals behaved, to predict weather. Elders and Inuit hunters say many of those traditional methods are unreliable now because the climate is warmer. The Inuit have also noticed new birds and insects, which normally would not live so far north, have moved into the Arctic. Even the ice the Inuit hunt on is melting, making it more dangerous for humans and for animals such as polar bears and seals.

*Polar bears use ice floes as platforms for hunting. Global warming is increasing the rate at which Arctic ice melts. With less ice to rest and hunt on, polar bears risk starving or drowning.*

5

# Feeling Hot, Hot, Hot

Scientists have kept track of the Earth's temperature for about 150 years. One way they keep track today is by making graphs or models in order to study the year to year differences in temperatures. The graphs tell scientists that there has been a long-term trend of rising temperatures over the past 150 years.

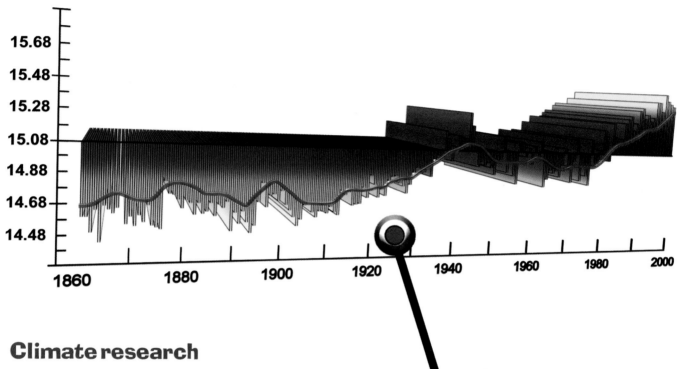

## Climate research

The people who produce temperature graphs work for centers of **climate research**. The graphs provide a record of changing temperature. They also provide information that **climatologists** use to compare computer models of future climate change. Models that did not include information on the air pollution produced by humans, did not match the temperature graphs very well. When pollution was included, the models closely matched the graphs. This convinced many **skeptical** scientists that the Earth was warming and fossil fuel use was a cause of global warming.

*The information, or data, used to make temperature graphs like this comes from many sources, including farmer's almanacs, magazines, and weather stations. The data is kept by climate scientists, called climatologists, who plot the graphs and study the changes. This graph shows how dramatically the average temperatures rise around 1970.*

1957

2004

# On the retreat

Other evidence that the Earth is getting warmer is the quick retreating or melting of glaciers. Glaciers are thick layers of compacted, or hardened, snow and ice that flow like slow rivers. Most glaciers are located in polar and mountainous regions. The Grinnell Glacier in Glacier National Park in Montana, has melted significantly in the past 50 years. The photos above show the glacier in 1957 (left) and 2004 (right). It is now a lake. Glaciers occupy about 10 percent of the world's land surface. Scientists fear rising average temperatures will melt Arctic and Antarctic glaciers, leading to a rise in sea level. This rise will change ocean habitats, weather systems, and endanger low-lying shorelines and ocean islands around the world.

## Climate modeling

Climatologists try to predict the future of the Earth's climate by using climatic models. Climatic models are computer models that take weather data and other information and calculate mathematically, what might take place in the future. The models predict things such as where rainfall will increase or decrease, and where growing seasons will become longer.

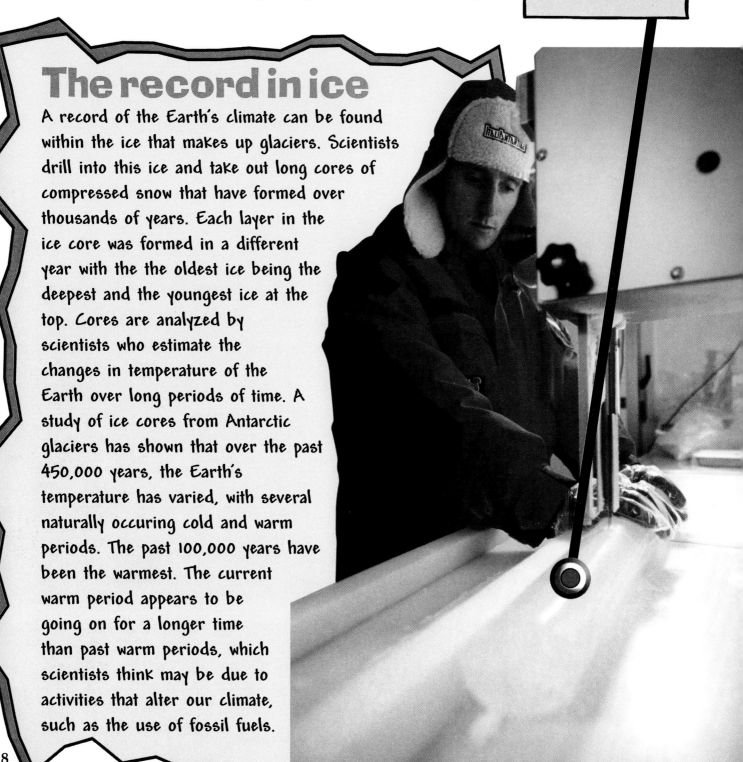

Some ice cores contain ice as old as 750,000 years.

# The record in ice

A record of the Earth's climate can be found within the ice that makes up glaciers. Scientists drill into this ice and take out long cores of compressed snow that have formed over thousands of years. Each layer in the ice core was formed in a different year with the the oldest ice being the deepest and the youngest ice at the top. Cores are analyzed by scientists who estimate the changes in temperature of the Earth over long periods of time. A study of ice cores from Antarctic glaciers has shown that over the past 450,000 years, the Earth's temperature has varied, with several naturally occuring cold and warm periods. The past 100,000 years have been the warmest. The current warm period appears to be going on for a longer time than past warm periods, which scientists think may be due to activities that alter our climate, such as the use of fossil fuels.

## Changing oceans

Scientists are finding that coral reefs near the equator in the Pacific Ocean are in danger because of higher ocean water temperatures and rising ocean levels. Coral reefs are important ocean **ecosystems** where thousands of fish and other marine animals live. Reefs are made up of the skeletons of many tiny organisms called polyps. The reefs grow near the ocean surface because they need sunlight. Coral reefs become "bleached," or lose their color, as colorful **algae** that live within the corals, die off due to the high water temperatures. Often, the polyps die too, because they need the algae to survive.

*This coral, located off the Maldive Islands in the Indian Ocean, has been bleached due to the loss of algae.*

## Arctic ecosystem change

In the Arctic, higher temperatures mean a change to the environment and ecosystems. Arctic ice breaks up, or melts, a full three weeks earlier than it did 30 years ago. The ice also takes longer to freeze in the fall. This late freeze and early thaw means polar bears have less time to hunt for food, and greater difficulty finding floating ice to rest on while hunting. When the ice is gone, polar bears must live on the land, where it is much more difficult for them to find the food that they need in order to live through the cold winters. They survive on the fat intake of hunting season and fast when the ice melts. Ringed seals use Arctic ice floes as calving grounds. With more melting ice, the calving season is shortened. Many animals that are well-suited to their habits today will not be able to survive as the world around them changes due to global warming.

*Pregnant polar bears are especially at risk with global warming, since they must survive longer on their stored fat.*

# Climate Science

Climatologists are scientists who study the long-term changes in weather that makes up the climate. They collect information on local weather conditions around the world and use that information to define the climate. Climatologists also try to understand what controls the climate of the Earth.

## Climate control

Sunlight provides the energy that warms the Earth. Climate depends on the amount of heat that the Sun's energy produces. When sunlight reaches the Earth's atmosphere, some of the energy is reflected back to space by clouds and tiny grains of dust and ice. The sunlight that makes it past the clouds reaches the surface of the Earth. Some of that light is reflected and some is absorbed to produce heat. The amount of sunlight, or energy, that is reflected depends on the color of the surface that it reaches, such as snow. Conditions in the atmosphere and at the Earth's surface control how much of the Sun's energy is available to warm the Earth.

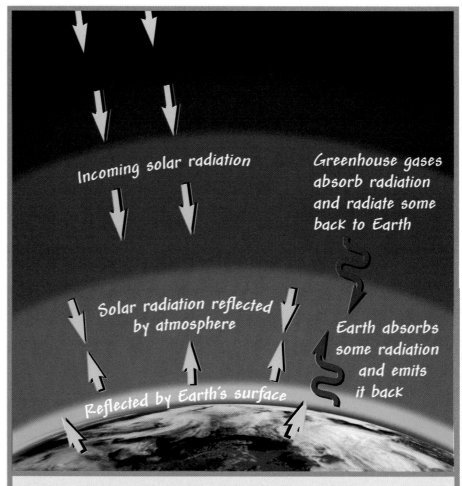

Incoming solar radiation

Greenhouse gases absorb radiation and radiate some back to Earth

Solar radiation reflected by atmosphere

Earth absorbs some radiation and emits it back

Reflected by Earth's surface

Some sunlight that reaches the Earth is reflected back to space. Sunlight that is not reflected by the Earth is absorbed and radiated back into the atmosphere as heat. Some of the heat remains in the atmosphere. The temperature of the Earth depends on how much heat remains in the atmosphere. The greenhouse gases act to trap the heat within the Earth's atmosphere, allowing the Earth to stay warm. If these gases were not present, the Earth would be much colder, and it would be difficult to support any life.

## Heating things up

Several gases that help keep the Earth warm occur naturally such as water vapor, carbon dioxide, methane, nitrous oxide, and ozone. These gases are produced by natural processes. Carbon dioxide, for example, is added to the atmosphere every time a volcano erupts. Water vapor is added to the atmosphere naturally through the water cycle, as water from the Earth's ocean, lakes, and rivers, **evaporates**. Other gases that are not naturally in the atmosphere, but are produced by humans, also keep the heat in. These gases include chlorofluorocarbons, which are used in refrigerators and air conditioners. Humans are also responsible for adding more of the "natural gases," such as carbon dioxide, methane, nitrous oxide, and ozone, to the atmosphere. All of these extra gases cause more heat to be trapped in the Earth's atmosphere. Most scientists believe these extra gases are what is causing global warming.

# Greenhouse Effect

The gases that keep the Earth warm are often called greenhouse gases. These gases act like the windows of a greenhouse because they allow the Sun's energy to pass through them and reach the Earth's surface where it is absorbed and radiated back as heat.

## Keeping things warm

The most important greenhouse gases in our atmosphere are water vapor, carbon dioxide, nitrous oxide, methane, and fluorocarbons. Greenhouse gases stop some of the Sun's heat from escaping the planet. Some of the heat does escape so that the Earth does not heat up endlessly. It is the **concentration** of greenhouse gases in the atmosphere that controls how much heat stays and how much escapes. Greenhouse gases are important because they determine the temperature of the Earth. Without greenhouse gases in our atmosphere the Earth would be too cold for us to live on and grow crops for food.

## Too much of a good thing

Naturally produced greenhouse gases, like carbon dioxide from volcanoes, have kept the Earth at a comfortable temperature over most of the past several billion years. The problem today is that the concentration of greenhouse gases is on the rise. Most scientists believe that this is because of the way humans live today.

*Vehicles contribute to a higher concentration of greenhouse gases by burning fossil fuels.*

## Our impact

Fossil fuels such as natural gas, oil, and coal are burned to heat homes in winter and produce the electricity needed to run air conditioners in the summer. Fossil fuels also provide the power needed to run everyday machines such as refrigerators, washers, and dryers. Fossil fuels are burned to create the energy used every day in homes, schools, factories, and office buildings. Burning fossil fuels produces carbon dioxide. Of the greenhouse gases that humans produce, carbon dioxide has the greatest impact on increasing global temperatures.

## Humans vs. nature

Humans produce about 150 times the amount of carbon dioxide that is produced by all of the volcanoes on Earth. Methane gas is released when humans drill wells for oil and gas, and as food and yard waste decays in landfills. Nitrous oxide is another greenhouse gas that humans add to the atmosphere when they make fertilizers that are needed to grow crops. Some of these gases also contribute to the destruction of the ozone layer, which helps keep damaging **radiation** from the Sun from reaching the Earth's surface.

*Air pollution has reached such a high level that it is difficult for the planet to recover.*

# Carbon cycle

Carbon dioxide that is added to the atmosphere is removed by natural processes over long periods of time. These natural processes are called the carbon cycle. Carbon dioxide is dissolved in rivers and oceans. Plants, such as trees, also take in carbon dioxide and use it to produce oxygen. Clear-cutting forests removes trees needed for the carbon cycle.

# Path of Destruction

**Many scientists are searching for evidence of the impact of global warming on Earth today, while others are trying to predict its effects in the future. As the global temperature rises, many changes will take place and no part of the Earth will be free from the effects of global warming.**

## Changing life on Earth

Global temperatures have increased by one degree Fahrenheit (0.6° Celsius) over the past 100 years. Many scientists think the average global temperature may rise by up to 10 degrees Fahrenheit (6° Celsius) before the end of the century. Such a rapid increase in global temperatures will change all life on Earth.

*Rising temperatures and smog from industrial and automobile pollution will make it difficult to breathe.*

## The evidence

Scientists have been studying global warming for decades. The United States National Academy of Science did its first major global warming study in 1979. It found that if carbon dioxide levels continued to increase, Earth's temperature would rise between two and a half and eight degrees Fahrenheit (1.4° and 4.4° Celsius). Many hundreds of studies on global warming have been done since that time. Most scientists agree that natural climate change cannot explain the rapid increase in temperatures.

## Habitat destruction

Through hundreds of studies, scientists already recognize that plants and animals that used to only live in warmer, southern parts of North America are moving further north. Near the poles, plants and animals adapted to cold temperatures are threatened by the higher temperatures. In Antarctica, some populations of penguins have already been reduced by one third due to the warmer conditions.

## Increased illness

The United Nations' World Health Organization reported 150,000 deaths were due to global warming in the year 2000. Many deaths were due to flooding or extreme summer heat waves. In 2003, a heat wave that affected much of Europe caused the deaths of over 21,000 people.

## Stronger storms?

Many scientists also believe global warming is responsible for an increase in extreme weather conditions such as hurricanes. Global warming has increased ocean surface temperatures in areas near the equator. Hurricanes use the warm ocean water as "fuel," building energy and wind through the exchange of warm water, vapor, and cool atmospheric air. In the northern hemisphere, Atlantic ocean hurricanes never dip south of the equator. Water temperatures are usually never high enough to produce the storms there. In March 2004, a hurricane struck the coast of Brazil and was the first southern Atlantic hurricane ever recorded. As the Earth and its oceans become warmer, storms will become longer and more powerful.

*Scientists warn of more floods and droughts as weather patterns are changed by global warming.*

## Wierd weather

The United Nations' World Meteorological Organization has said there will be many changes in weather patterns worldwide. Some areas will experience long periods of drought from lack of rain. This will reduce the amount of food that can be grown. Other areas will become much wetter than they were in the past. In the central United States over the month of May 2003, 562 tornadoes were reported, the largest number ever recorded for that month. Tornadoes are violent, rotating windstorms that form when cold, dry air meets warm, moist air. Global warming changes weather patterns and creates the conditions needed for tornadoes.

As permafrost melts, ice turns to water and the ground becomes unstable. The permafrost zone includes the Arctic areas of the United States, Canada, and Europe. This house in Fairbanks, Alaska, has sunk because of melting permafrost.

# Thawing the permafrost

Permafrost is permanently frozen ground that is found in polar regions of the world. These vast frozen areas are beginning to thaw as the Earth becomes warmer. In Siberia, in eastern Asia, 386,102 square miles (one million square kilometers) of permafrost that has lasted for 11,000 years has begun to melt. As the ground in this region melts, the greenhouse gas, methane, that is naturally trapped in the soil will be released into the atmosphere, causing more warming.

## Glacial retreat

One of the most dramatic changes that scientists have witnessed has been the rapid retreat of glaciers in high mountain regions. At high **altitudes**, cold temperatures have allowed glaciers to grow and advance for centuries. When melting takes place at a greater rate than snow and ice accumulates, the front of the glacier will retreat. Over the past 100 years, glaciers all over the world have become smaller as rising temperatures cause them to melt. In Tanzania, Mount Kilimanjaro's glacial cap has shrunk to a small fraction of its original size over the last 100 years. Scientists believe the 12,000-year-old glacier will be gone entirely by the year 2020. In North America, Glacier National Park, in Montana, had over 150 glaciers in 1850, but the number has dwindled to about 35 glaciers today.

*Workers roll out an insulating cover on a glacier in the Swiss Alps. The cover protects the ice from melting in the summer heat.*

Some scientists believe diseases are spreading into new areas as the global temperature increases. Many serious diseases may be caught from the bites of insects such as mosquitoes. In cooler areas of the world, frost kills mosquitoes and their eggs so that they cannot pass on diseases, such as malaria, to humans. With global warming, disease-carrying mosquitoes are now spreading over wider areas.

# Our Climate History

Some scientists dismiss global warming by saying the current warming trend is just normal climate fluctuation. Over the past 4.5 billion years, there have been periods when the Earth's overall climate was much colder and times when it was warmer.

## Growing glaciers

Some Earth scientists believe that about 700 million years ago, the Earth was almost entirely covered with ice. The glaciers advanced, or grew, from the poles toward the equator when the Earth became colder. It has been estimated that the average global temperature was roughly -58° Fahrenhiet (-50° Celsius). As the ice masses grew, their surface of bright ice reflected a larger proportion of the sunlight. That sunlight was not absorbed by the Earth to create heat. With so much of the Sun's energy being reflected, the Earth became even colder, causing the glaciers to advance further from the polar regions toward the equator.

*About 700 million years ago, the Earth was much colder than it is today. Greenhouse gases, such as carbon dioxide from erupting volcanoes, raised global temperatures to 104° Fahrenheit (40° Celsius) and forced the glaciers into retreat.*

## Melting snowball

Geologists are scientists who study the Earth and the rocks and minerals that make up our planet. Many geologists are especially interested in the history of the Earth. They have found 700 million-year-old rocks near the Earth's equator. The rocks were formed by the ancient glaciers that covered the Earth. This is one example of scientific evidence that the Earth had frozen over in the past. Scientists spent many years trying to determine what caused the planet to become warm enough to melt those massive glaciers. The answer lies in volcanoes. Millions of years ago, volcanoes erupted beneath the giant sheets of ice. The eruptions released gases from deep within the Earth. Scientists estimate that it would have taken millions of years for the glaciers to melt away.

# Continental glaciation

Over the past few million years, the Earth has undergone repeated periods of time, or cycles, when glaciers have advanced. During periods of relatively cold global temperature, glaciers advance, or grow, from the poles. They advance toward the equator to cause what is called continental glaciation, or enormous masses of ice that cover entire continents. These periods of glaciation are also sometimes called "ice ages." Ice ages end when the glaciers retreat, or shrink, back toward the poles as the global climate becomes warmer. The cycles of colder, followed by warmer, global temperatures are thought to be due to changes in the amount of energy from the Sun that reaches the Earth. Every 100,000 years, the position of the Earth's orbit around the Sun encourages continental glaciation. This cycle of continental glaciation has been followed by periods of warming, where the glaciers melted, or receded. Scientists believe that these cycles are related to changes in the rotation of the Earth and its orbit around the Sun. These cycles affect how much energy is received in different parts of the planet, especially near the poles, over the course of a year.

*A volcano under the Vatnajokull glacier in Iceland spews steam and magma. The underground volcano erupted in 1996 and caused part of the glacier to rapidly melt and flood parts of the island.*

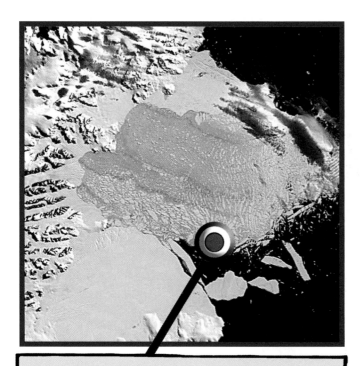

The Larsen B ice shelf, a large floating ice mass on the eastern side of Antarctica, shattered and separated from the continent due to global warming In 2002. The ice shelf existed since the last Ice Age 12,000 years ago.

## Colder and warmer

Relatively brief periods of colder temperatures have taken place in the past. Many volcanic eruptions added large volumes of carbon dioxide to the atmosphere, causing a greenhouse effect that warmed the Earth over long periods of time. Some volcanic eruptions also added large volumes of ash and other material that had the opposite effect on Earth's temperature. During an explosive eruption, dust-size ash is ejected high up into the Earth`s atmosphere where it is driven by the wind and circles the Earth. This ash, and other material, acts to shade the Earth from sunlight, reducing the amount of the Sun's energy that reaches the Earth's surface to create heat. This volcanic ash often remained in the atmosphere for several years, cooling the Earth.

In 1991, Mount Pinatubo, in the Phillipines, erupted and sent large volumes of ash into the atmosphere. The next year, northern hemisphere temperatures were reduced.

# When dinosaurs roamed

About 100 million years ago, during a period of time that geologists call the "Cretaceous Period," Earth was much warmer than it is today. Scientists estimate that the Earth's average temperature was nine degrees Fahrenheit (five degrees Celsius) warmer than it is today. That temperature was warm enough to melt the polar glaciers and helped cause sea levels to be higher than any other time in history. Tropical plants and animals lived much farther from the equator due to the higher temperatures. Scientists are not certain why the Cretaceous Period was so warm, but it may have been due to volcanoes. Volcanoes were especially active during this period. Volcanic eruptions added very large amounts of carbon dioxide to the Earth's atomosphere and the resulting greenhouse effect is thought to have led to the particularly high temperatures. The Earth became cooler again toward the end of the Cretaceous Period as volcanic activity became less and the amount of carbon dioxide in the atmosphere decreased. This reduced the greenhouse effect and let more and more heat escape from the Earth.

# Warming the Oceans

As the temperature of the Earth's atmosphere rises, the temperature of the world's oceans does as well, especially the waters near the surface. This warming will affect the plants and animals that live in the oceans as well as weather patterns that are influenced by the ocean's surface water temperature.

## Positive feedback process

Phytoplankton are tiny plants that are a food source for many animals that live in the Earth's oceans. Phytoplankton are very sensitive to water temperature. When the water is cooler, it is rich in **nutrients** that are needed for the phytoplankton to thrive and grow in numbers. When ocean water is warmer, the phytoplankton are fewer in numbers. Phytoplankton are also important because they use large volumes of carbon dioxide that would otherwise be released into the atmosphere. With global warming, scientists expect that the reduction in the phytoplankton as a food supply, may result in the loss of millions of animals throughout the world's oceans. With warmer oceans and fewer phytoplankton, carbon dioxide will continue to increase in the atmosphere and further add to global warming. Scientists call this process positive feedback. As the Earth becomes warmer, environmental changes take place that will cause even further warming.

*The North American right whale is one of the most endangered of all whales. Only 300 to 350 of the whales exist today and scientists believe the population will further decrease with the loss of phytoplankton, the right whale's major food source.*

## Rising sea level

The water that is released from melting glaciers flows through rivers to the oceans of the world, causing the level of the world's oceans to rise. Rising sea levels erode shorelines, swamp low-lying islands, and endanger many animal species. Scientists predict that as global warming continues, sea level may rise by almost 20 inches (50 centimeters) by the end of the century. How much sea level rises depends on how warm the temperatures become and how quickly the glaciers melt. Most of the world's glaciers are found on Greenland and Antarctica. The glaciers of Greenland are right now melting at a faster rate than has ever been recorded.

*As sea levels rise, more people in low-lying islands and coastal areas will become global warming refugees. A cemetery on the Marshall Islands atoll, or coral reef, of Majro, has been destroyed by high sea levels and wave erosion.*

Unusually warm weather in Antarctica forces a Gentoo penguin chick to sleep on a rock.

## Bye-bye habitat

Shoreline areas and ocean marshes are home to many species of birds, animals, and insects. Flooding destroys their delicate habitats. Sea turtles lay their eggs on South American beaches threatened by rising water levels. The turtles are further threatened by the warming of their nesting areas. Since temperature determines the sex of turtles, warm nests produce only female offspring, leaving the turtles without enough males to reproduce. Human populations are also affected by rising ocean levels. The entire population of the low-lying south Pacific island of Carteret, at 980 people, was forced to move when rising waters swamped their island. The entire island will be under water by 2015.

# The Toll on Life

As the planet continues to become warmer, the changes that take place will affect all living things. A warming Earth will bring more natural disasters, sickness, and even wars over resources and territory.

## Economic impact

Translating temperature change into its impact on the world is difficult. Some changes have already occured and some are expected in the future. Climate scientists check their research models against historic data and the work of other scientists. The people who examine the economic impact of global warming also develop models that tell them what is likely to happen if climate change continues. Their predictions are not good. Recent studies suggest that the world economy will shrink by 20 percent if nothing is done about global warming.

## Changing ways of life

Economists study the production and consumption, or use, of goods. Many economists believe everything from farming to travel and shipping will be affected by global warming. Global warming droughts in some areas of the world have already changed the way people live. Scientists think more severe droughts in the future will destroy crops and force people to move. Economists believe the impact of the destroyed crops will be higher food prices and an **influx** of people from farms to cities. One global warming report estimates that flooding from glacial melt could **displace** up to 100 million people worldwide.

*Recent global warming droughts have forced many to abandon their traditional ways of life. These members of Kenya's Massai people, who are suffering global warming-created droughts, call attention to climate change at a United Nations Conference.*

Stop Climate Injustice

## Environmental refugees

Refugees are people who are forced to flee their homes because their lives are threatened by war or disasters. Global warming has already created refugees in many parts of the world. In Africa, the Masai people are **semi-nomadic** cattle herders in Kenya and Tanzania. They bring their animals to graze on grasslands at different times of the year. Several years of severe droughts, which experts believe are a result of changing weather patterns due to global warming, have dried up the grazing lands. The Masai can no longer predict when the annual rains will come and many of their animals have died from lack of food. Wealth is measured in cattle for the Masai. Some Masai have lost so many cattle they have become poor. They have had to move to cities to take jobs there, leaving behind a way of life they have lived for centuries. Global warming is forcing the Masai to adapt very quickly to another way of life.

A Masai herder leads his cattle across a major street in downtown Nairobi, Kenya, during a severe drought in 2000. The drought forced the Masai to find water and pasture for their cattle in the country's biggest city. Global warming puts pressure on governments to provide food, housing, and new jobs for displaced people.

# Global warming wars?

Parts of the world will become hotter and dryer due to global warming, while other parts will be flooded. The movement of large numbers of environmental refugees to new areas could lead to fighting as scarce food and other resources must be shared among many. Clean drinking water and food will become commodities that not everyone can afford.

*The land will change in ways that will make it impossible for the people who live there to stay. They will become environmental refugees who move into other areas where people already live.*

## Food production

Many scientists believe global warming will have an impact on food production but the total amount of food that is produced will not decrease rapidly. The changes and economic impacts will not be even around the world. Some cold areas, where growing food crops is now difficult, will become warmer so that the amount of food produced will increase.

*Lack of rain leaves the ground parched between the rows of a North Dakota corn field. Global warming will change the weather patterns, making some areas more prone to droughts.*

# Lessons Learned

Global warming is showing us that we cannot live our lives without concern for the environment. The Earth's atmosphere is not vast enough to accept large volumes of greenhouse gases without noticeable effect. Humans must consider the well-being of the Earth in order to ensure our own well-being.

## Working together

Global warming is one of the greatest challenges that has ever faced the human species. It will affect the entire planet and will require cooperation between countries in order to withstand its impacts and to reduce its long-term effects. No matter what is done, global warming will not be brought to a rapid stop. The Earth will continue to become warmer in the future because global warming is caused by the way people live today.

## Searching for alternatives

People can make changes to slow the progress of global warming by reducing, reusing, recycling, and using alternate fuels to replace the fossil fuels used today. Governments can play their part by passing laws that require industry and people to **conserve** and use products that do not further harm the environment.

*The United States produces more greenhouse gases than any other country on Earth.*

# The Kyoto Protocol

The Kyoto Protocol is a United Nations climate change agreement made by a number of countries aimed at reducing the amount of greenhouse gases produced around the world. The agreement was made in 1997 and it came into effect in 2005, with 169 different participating countries. The agreement aims to reduce the amount of greenhouse gases to the level that humans produced in the year 1990. The countries that ratified, or confirmed support for, the protocol are responsible for passing their own laws and regulations that reduce greenhouse gas emissions. They can be penalized for not meeting their targets. The agreement has been criticized for both not being tough enough, and being too difficult to bring about. Many scientists believe reducing greenhouse gases will not stop global warming altogether but it will slow its rate.

Walkers, bike riders, and people who use mass, or public transit to get around are helping the planet by using less fossil fuels. Cutting emissions now gives us more time to prepare for the future.

The governments of The United States and Australia signed the Kyoto Protocol but did not ratify it. They prefer to develop their own global warming prevention plans. Some other countries, such as Canada, ratified the agreement, but have not made a great effort to reduce emissions.

# Do Your Part!

An environmental footprint is a measure of your impact on the planet. It is determined by how you live your life, including the amount of energy you use, how you eat, travel, and what you purchase. Try the footprint quiz to determine your footprint. Follow the tips for reducing your impact on the Earth to see how you can do your part to reduce global warming.

## 1

1) Do you walk or bike to school? Yes = 0 points.

2) Do you use public transit or are you bussed to school?
Yes = 1 point

3) Are you driven to school in a car?
Yes = 3 points

Vehicles use fossil fuels that are the single worst contributors to greenhouse gases. Public transit brings many people to the same place while single vehicles transport very few.

## 2

Do you eat more than one item of packaged food, processed food, or food imported from another country each day?

Yes = 2 points     No = 0 points

Packaged, processed, and imported food uses more energy to produce and deliver to market, which adds to greenhouse gases.

**3**  Do you turn the lights off in a room after leaving it?

Yes = 1 point

No = 2 points

*Wasting energy uses more fossil fuels.*

**4**  How many times do you and your family fly each year?

Never = 0 points

Once or twice = 2 points

More than twice = 3 points

*Flying puts an enormous amount of carbon dioxide into the atmosphere, adding to the greenhouse effect.*

**5** Tally up your points.

1 to 2 points =  1 footprint Very Good!

3 to 4 points =  2 footprints Good!

5, 6, and above =  three footprints Needs Improvement

Check out the tips below to see how you can improve your footprint.

# How you can help

We have to change the way we live in order to reduce our energy needs. Using energy produces greenhouse gases. Be aware that how you live your life has an impact on the planet and on other people and animals that live on Earth. Pass these tips on conserving energy on to your family:

1) Use less electricity by turning off lights when they are not needed and reducing the temperature in homes, schools, and offices in winter.

2) Use air conditioners only when absolutely necessary. Turning the air up only makes the planet hotter.

3) Replace your regular light bulbs with energy-efficient ones like the one shown in this box.

4) Drive less and make fewer unnecessary trips by car and by air. Drive a more fuel-efficient car.

5) Eat food grown locally when possible. The further food has to travel, the more fossil fuels that must be used.

# Glossary

**algae** Ocean life forms, from tiny organisms to giant kelp, that other ocean life feed on

**altitude** The height of something above a reference point

**atmosphere** The mix of gases surrounding the Earth that are held in place by gravity

**climate research** The study of weather conditions and what affects the conditions in an area over a long period of time

**climatologist** The weather conditions in a specific area averaged over time

**commodity** A good that is bought and sold

**concentration** The strength or level of something. A high concentration of ink in water means that there is a lot of ink in the water

**conserve** To use or manage wisely or preserve

**displace** To move or take the place of something

**ecosystems** A community of organisms, such as plants and animals, and the environments they live in

**evaporate** To change from a liquid to a vapor or gas

**fossil fuels** Fuels such as coal, oil, and natural gas, that formed from the remains of plants and animals that lived millions of years ago. Fossil fuels are used to power vehicles. Their emissions are harmful to the environment

**glaciers** Huge masses of compacted, or hardened, ice and snow that flow like rivers down mountains and the Earth's poles

**greenhouse gases** Naturally occuring gases in the atmosphere, such as carbon dioxide. Fossil fuel emissions increase the amount of greenhouse gases in the atmosphere

**habitats** The environments where animals naturally live

**influx** Inflow, or the act of flowing in

**malaria** A disease passed on by infected mosquitoes to the people they bite. Malaria can make a person seriously ill

**nutrient** Something that is a source of nourishment for proper growth

**polar ice caps** The ice glaciers at the North and South Poles

**radiation** Rays of energy emitted from the Sun

**semi-nomadic** People who travel parts of the year to bring their herds of animals to pasture lands

**skeptical** Showing doubt or questioning a statement of fact

# Index

**Printed in the U.S.A.**